Contents

My Body

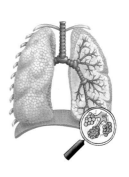

People and Places

The Earth

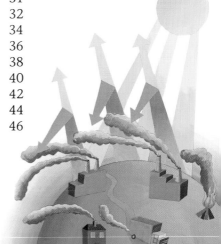

Animals and plants

Science

4

Technology

The Universe

OXFORD
First Book of
FACTS

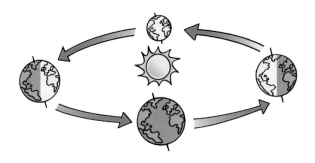

OXFORD
UNIVERSITY PRESS

OXFORD
UNIVERSITY PRESS

Great Clarendon Street, Oxford OX2 6DP

Oxford University Press is a department of the University of Oxford.
It furthers the University's objective of excellence in research, scholarship,
and education by publishing worldwide in

Oxford New York

Athens Auckland Bangkok Bogotá Buenos Aires Calcutta
Cape Town Chennai Dar es Salaam Delhi Florence Hong Kong Istanbul
Karachi Kuala Lumpur Madrid Melbourne Mexico City Mumbai
Nairobi Paris São Paulo Singapore Taipei Tokyo Toronto Warsaw

with associated companies in Berlin Ibadan

Oxford is a registered trade mark of Oxford University Press
in the UK and in certain other countries

© Oxford University Press 2000

First published 2000

British Library Cataloguing in Publication Data available

Paperback ISBN 0-19-910685-1

1 3 5 7 9 10 8 6 4 2

Printed in Hong Kong

My Body

Skin and hair

✳ Your skin makes you waterproof, keeps out germs and stops you getting too hot or cold.

Your skin colour depends on how much melanin (dark colouring) you have. Melanin helps to protect the skin from sunburn, so people with pale skin (less melanin) burn more easily than dark-skinned people.

✳ Your skin has two main layers – an outer layer of dead cells called the epidermis, and an inner layer of living cells called the dermis.

✳ Your hair and nails are growing all the time. If you do not cut your hair, it will normally grow to about a metre long, then stop.

hair

epidermis

dermis

pore (hole)

sweat gland

blood vessel

nerve ending

The senses

❋ We have five senses – sight, hearing, smell, taste and touch.

❋ You see with your eyes. Your eye lets in light through a round 'window', called the pupil. Behind the pupil is a lens. This makes a picture of what you are looking at on the back of the eye.

light rays

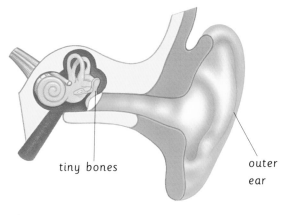

tiny bones

outer ear

❋ You hear with your ears. Sounds are vibrations in the air. Your ears gather sounds from outside, and tiny bones inside your ear make them louder.

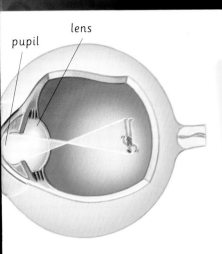

pupil

lens

Blind people read books which have a special kind of 'writing' called Braille. Each letter has a code of dots, which stick up slightly from the page. Readers can feel the dots with their fingers.

7

* You smell with your nose. Smells in the air come in through your nose as you breathe.

* Your tongue tells you whether food is sweet, salty, bitter or sour. Your sense of smell also helps you to taste things. When you cannot smell properly, many foods taste similar.

* You sense touch through nerve endings in your skin. You can sense if things are hot or cold, soft, hard, sharp, wet or dry.

Bones and muscles

✳ Your skeleton is made up of more than 200 bones. It holds up your body and gives it shape. Your skeleton also protects the soft parts of your body, such as your brain.

skull

✳ Bones are hard on the outside, but there are softer, living cells inside. Some big bones, like your thigh bone, are filled with bone marrow. This is a soft tissue that makes new cells for your blood.

ribs

hard bone

pelvis

thigh bone

bone marrow

✳ Joints are the places where your bones meet. Strong cords called ligaments hold the bones together. Your shoulder and hip joints can move in any direction. Other joints, like your elbows and knees, can only bend in one direction.

triceps

biceps

Your eye muscles tighten or relax more than 100,000 times every day!

✳ You have more than 600 muscles in your body. Many of them are attached to your bones. Together, your muscles and bones move your body.

stomach muscles

✳ As a muscle shortens, it pulls on the bones it is fastened to, making them move. Muscles such as the biceps and triceps in your arm only work when you tell them to. Other muscles, such as the ones that help you breathe, work even when you are asleep!

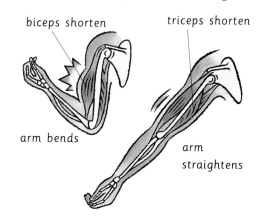

biceps shorten

triceps shorten

arm bends

arm straightens

Lungs and breathing

✳ You use your lungs to breathe. The air you breathe in contains oxygen, which you need to stay alive. The air you breathe out contains carbon dioxide, which you want to get rid of.

✳ Your ribs form a protective cage around your lungs. Below them is a muscle called the diaphragm. Muscles between the ribs can move them either up and outwards, or down and inwards.

✳ When you breathe in, the diaphragm tightens and your ribs move outwards. This makes your chest and lungs expand, sucking in air through your mouth.

lungs

ribs

diaphragm

breathing in

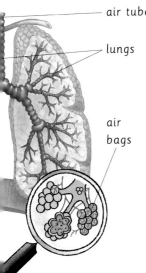

air tube from mouth

lungs

air bags

✳ Your lungs are full of tiny air bags, surrounded by very thin blood vessels. Oxygen from the air you breathe in passes through these bags and into your blood. At the same time, carbon dioxide passes out of your blood into the lungs, and is breathed out.

✳ When you breathe out, the diaphragm relaxes and the ribs move down. Your chest gets smaller, and air is squeezed out of your lungs.

breathing out

When you are asleep, you breathe slowly and gently. Your body is still, so it only needs a small amount of oxygen. When you run about, your body needs more oxygen, so you breathe more quickly.

The heart and the blood system

✳ Blood carries food and oxygen to all parts of your body. It travels along tubes called blood vessels.

✳ Arteries carry blood filled with oxygen from the lungs. This blood is bright red.

✳ Veins carry blood filled with carbon dioxide and other waste materials back to the lungs. This blood is dark red.

✳ Capillaries are tiny blood vessels connecting the arteries and the veins.

capillaries

lungs

heart

vein

artery

An adult has about 4–5 litres of blood, and about 100,000 kilometres of blood vessels. A blood cell takes about one minute to flow round the body.

The human heart . . about 70 times a minute, more after exercise or if you are angry, afraid or excited. An elephant's heart beats about 25–30 times a minute. The heart of a small bird beats about 300 times a minute.

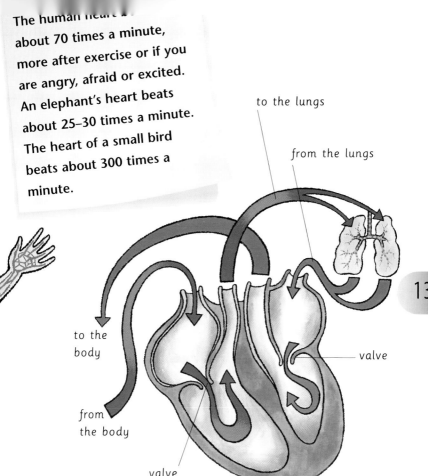

to the lungs

from the lungs

to the body

from the body

valve

valve

✳ The heart is a strong muscle. One side pumps blood to the lungs, where it receives oxygen. The other side takes this blood and pumps it round the body. Blood flows round the body in one direction. Small flaps, called valves, in the heart and veins prevent the blood from flowing the wrong way.

The brain and nerves

✳ Your brain is inside your head. It controls your whole body and nearly everything you do. Your brain sorts and stores information so that you can think, learn and remember. It sends out orders to your body about speaking and moving.

✳ Different parts of the brain have different jobs. Each of your senses, for instance, has its own area of the brain. But all parts of the brain are involved in thinking and memory.

✳ Your brain is connected to the rest of your body by cords called nerves. These carry messages between the brain and the body. For example, some nerves carry messages from your brain to your muscles, telling you how to move.

moving

touching

seeing

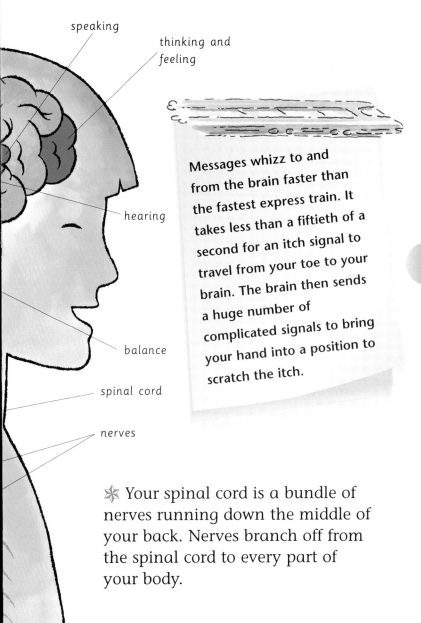

speaking

thinking and feeling

hearing

balance

spinal cord

nerves

Messages whizz to and from the brain faster than the fastest express train. It takes less than a fiftieth of a second for an itch signal to travel from your toe to your brain. The brain then sends a huge number of complicated signals to bring your hand into a position to scratch the itch.

15

✳ Your spinal cord is a bundle of nerves running down the middle of your back. Nerves branch off from the spinal cord to every part of your body.

The digestive system

✳ The substances your body needs from food are called nutrients. Digestion is the way your body gets nutrients from food, and gets rid of any waste.

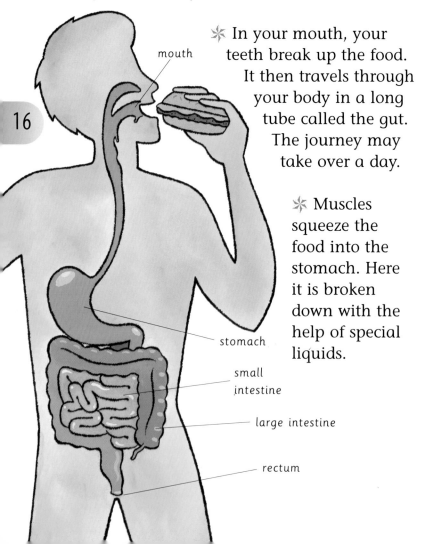

✳ In your mouth, your teeth break up the food. It then travels through your body in a long tube called the gut. The journey may take over a day.

✳ Muscles squeeze the food into the stomach. Here it is broken down with the help of special liquids.

mouth

stomach

small intestine

large intestine

rectum

enamel

hole

nerve

Your teeth are covered on the outside in hard enamel. Sugary foods and fizzy drinks can damage the enamel and make holes in your teeth. If a hole reaches the nerve, you will get toothache. So keep your teeth clean!

✳ In the small intestine all the useful parts of the food pass into your blood. The parts that are left are waste. This goes into the large intestine and leaves the body through the rectum.

17

✳ Blood carrying the useful parts of food comes from your intestines to the liver. The liver stores some food, and turns the rest into nutrients that the body cells can use.

liver

kidney

bladder

✳ Your kidneys help to keep your blood clean. They take out any unwanted material from the blood and turn it into urine (wee). This is stored in your bladder until you go to the toilet.

Pregnancy and birth

✳ A baby is made from an egg from a mother, and a sperm from a father. An egg is smaller than a full stop. A sperm is even tinier, and looks a bit like a tadpole.

✳ The father has lots of sperms. They travel into the mother's body until they reach the egg. Then one sperm joins with the egg, to make the first cell of the new baby.

✳ The new baby starts to grow in the mother's uterus. The egg splits to make two cells, then four, then eight, and so on. The growing baby gets food from its mother through a tube called the umbilical cord.

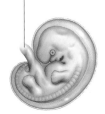

umbilical cord

baby at six weeks

uterus

400,000 babies are born every day. That's 255 every minute!

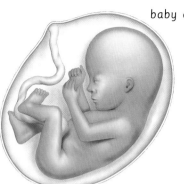

baby at three months

✳ The baby is fully formed after just three months. But it is still very tiny.

umbilical cord

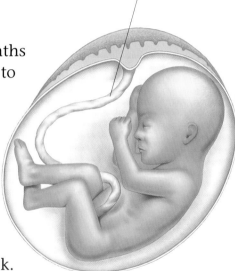

✳ After nine months the baby is ready to be born. Muscles in the mother's uterus push the baby out, usually head first. The umbilical cord is cut. The newborn baby feeds on milk.

19

baby at seven months

✳ Babies learn quickly. Soon they can smile and laugh, grip with their hands, roll over and make noises. By the age of one, many are learning to walk and can say a few words.

Illness and health

✳ Most illnesses are caused by tiny living things called germs. Germs carry diseases from one person to another. The germs get passed on when people touch, cough or sneeze.

20

✳ If you are ill you may need to see a doctor, who can give you medicine. If you are very ill you may have to go to hospital.

Keeping your body clean helps to get rid of germs. Always wash your hands after using the toilet, and before you touch any food.

✳ If you keep clean, exercise and eat the right foods, you are less likely to become ill. Running, swimming and cycling are all good kinds of exercise.

People and Places

Families

✳ A family is a group of people who are related to each other. They care for each other and share money, food and housework.

✳ There are many different kinds of family. In some families only one parent lives with the children. Other families are very big, with children, parents, grandparents, aunts, uncles and cousins all living together.

grandmother

grandmother

grandfather

grandfather

uncle

aunt

aunt

father

mother

uncle

Can you make a family tree? Ask older people in your family to help you.

brother

me

sister

cousins

Homes

✳ Homes come in all shapes and sizes. They are built from many different materials.

✳ Tall apartment blocks in big cities are built in steel and concrete, with large glass windows. In some hot countries, people live in small shelters that shade them from the sun.

✳ Bedouin people travel from place to place with their animals. They need a home that is easy to move.

Bedouin tent

houses

car park

offices

✳ Log houses in Russia are made from wood, cut from the forests all around.

✳ A village is a small group of homes. Some villages grow into towns, and some towns into big cities.

✳ In towns and cities, thousands of people live and work close together. Big cities like Tokyo, London and Mexico City are busy and noisy, with many shops, offices, houses, cars, buses, trains and factories.

buses

hospital

market

People at work

✳ People work to provide food, clothes and a home for themselves and their families.

✳ In some parts of the world people catch their own food and make their own clothes. They gather fruit and vegetables and hunt animals. Other people, like fishermen, catch food to sell.

Japanese fishermen

✳ Farmers use the land to grow food. They sow crops, such as wheat and rice. Or they raise animals – cattle, pigs, sheep, goats and chickens – for meat, milk, eggs or wool.

Artists have special skills that they use in their work. Musicians play their instruments to entertain us, actors take part in plays, and visual artists draw and paint.

Some people make things for others to buy. Craft workers make beautiful objects such as clay pots or woollen rugs. In factories, people use machines to make everything from cars to toothbrushes.

weaving rugs in India

Many workers do not make or grow anything. They work in offices, or sell things in shops. Or they may do jobs that help other people, like nurses, police officers, firefighters, or bus and train drivers.

firefighter

Food

✳ Food gives you energy to work, play and think. The main substances your body needs from food are carbohydrates, proteins and fats.

The range of foods that you eat is called your diet. A healthy diet provides the right nutrients in the right amounts. It includes plenty of cereals – such as rice, bread or pasta – and fruit and vegetables.

high-protein foods

✳ Your body needs protein to grow. Foods that are high in protein include fish, meat, milk, beans and eggs.

✳ Carbohydrate foods, such as bread, pasta and potatoes, give you energy.

carbohydrate foods

✳ Fat gives you energy and also keeps you warm. Butter, milk and cheese are rich in fat.

fatty foods

Japanese raw fish

✳ You also need small amounts of vitamins and minerals to stay healthy. Vegetables, fruits, eggs, milk and fish contain plenty of vitamins and minerals.

groundnut stew

✳ People around the world eat very different meals.

✳ In Europe and North America, foods like pizza and beefburgers are popular. Japanese people eat a lot of fish, often served raw. Groundnut (peanut) stew with fufu is an African dish – chicken in a peanut sauce, with vegetable dumplings.

fufu

pizza

Religion

✳ There are many different religions in the world. The five biggest are Christianity, Islam, Hinduism, Judaism and Buddhism.

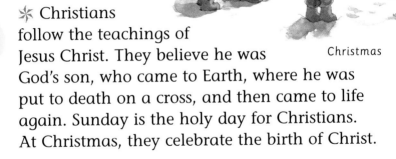

Christmas

✳ Christians follow the teachings of Jesus Christ. They believe he was God's son, who came to Earth, where he was put to death on a cross, and then came to life again. Sunday is the holy day for Christians. At Christmas, they celebrate the birth of Christ.

✳ Followers of Islam (Muslims) believe in one God, Allah, and follow the teachings of the Prophet Muhammad. Muslims are taught to pray five times each day, give money to the poor, travel at least once to the holy city of Mecca, and fast (eat no daytime food) for one month (Ramadan) each year. At the end of Ramadan, they celebrate.

end of Ramadan

✳ Judaism is the religion of the Jews. Saturday is the Jewish day of rest. They go to pray in a synagogue, their place of worship. Hannukah is the Jewish festival of lights.

lighting Hannukah candles

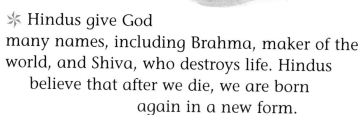

29

✳ Hindus give God many names, including Brahma, maker of the world, and Shiva, who destroys life. Hindus believe that after we die, we are born again in a new form.

✳ Buddhists have no gods. They follow the teachings of an Indian prince, who became known as Buddha. Buddhists spend time each day meditating, when they sit still and relax their minds.

Sport

✳ There are hundreds of different sports and games all over the world. Sports such as football and volleyball can be played almost anywhere. But others, such as skiing or motor racing, need special equipment.

30

skiing

Football is a very old game. A kind of football was probably played in China over 2,000 years ago. Soccer (association football) is the most popular game in the world.

✳ You do some sports on your own, like swimming. But many sports are played in teams.

The Earth

Day and night

✳ The Earth is a huge ball of rock that spins round in space. It takes 24 hours to turn all the way round. On the side where the Sun shines, it is day. On the side facing away from the Sun, it is night.

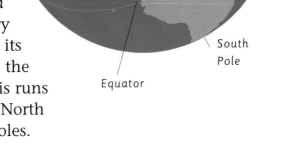

North Pole

axis

DAY

NIGHT

South Pole

Equator

✳ The Earth spins around an imaginary line through its centre called the axis. The axis runs through the North and South Poles.

✳ The Equator is an imaginary line that runs around the middle of the Earth.

The world

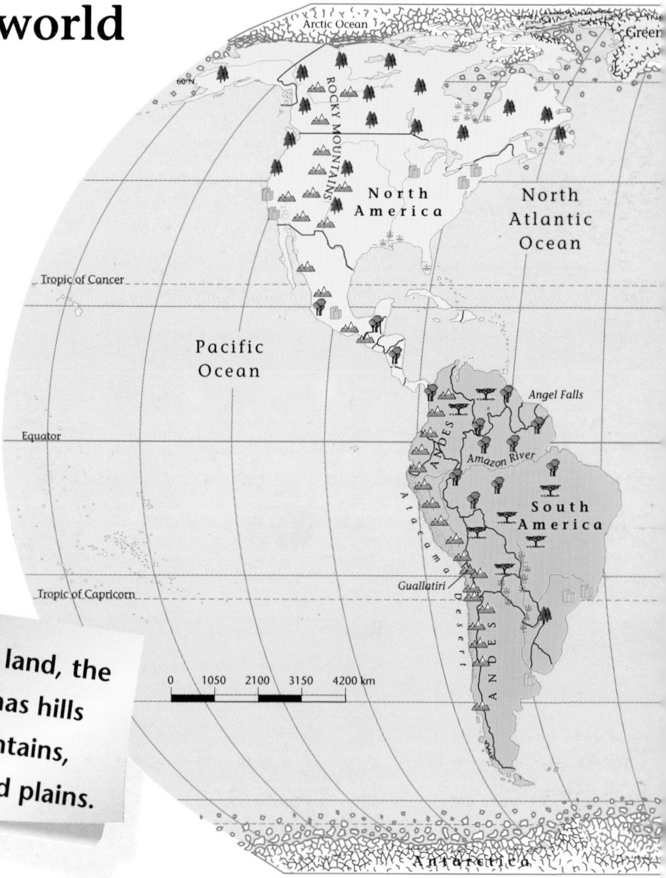

Arctic Ocean
60°N
ROCKY MOUNTAINS
North America
North Atlantic Ocean
Tropic of Cancer
Pacific Ocean
Angel Falls
Equator
ANDES
Amazon River
South America
Atacama Desert
Guallatiri
Tropic of Capricorn
0 1050 2100 3150 4200 km
ANDES
Antarctica

Like the land, the sea bed has hills and mountains, valleys and plains.

✳ All the land on Earth is divided up into seven big areas called 'continents'. These are Africa, Asia, Antarctica, Europe, North America, South America and Oceania.

✳ Nearly two-thirds of the Earth's surface is covered by oceans – the Atlantic, the Pacific, the Indian, the Arctic and the Southern Oceans.

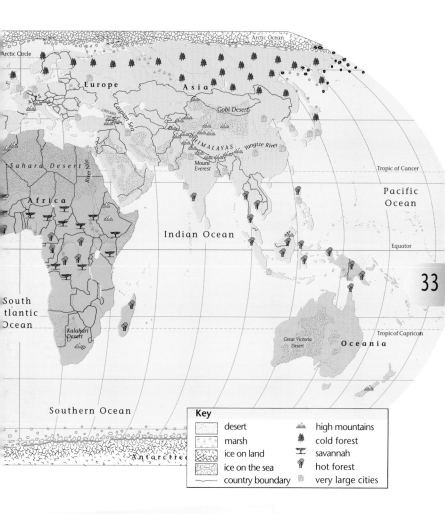

Arctic Ocean

Arctic Circle

Europe   Asia

ALPS

CAUCASUS

Caspian Sea

Gobi Desert

Sahara Desert

River Nile

HIMALAYAS

Yangtze River

Mount Everest

Tropic of Cancer

Africa

Pacific Ocean

Indian Ocean

Equator

South Atlantic Ocean

Kalahari Desert

Great Victoria Desert

Oceania

Tropic of Capricorn

33

Southern Ocean

Antarctica

Key

desert		high mountains	
marsh		cold forest	
ice on land		savannah	
ice on the sea		hot forest	
country boundary		very large cities	

- Asia is the largest continent.
- The Pacific is the biggest ocean.
- Mount Everest is the highest mountain.
- The Nile is the longest river.
- Greenland is the largest island.
- The Sahara is the biggest desert.

The Earth's rocks and atmosphere

✳ The Earth's outer layer is called the crust. The crust is made of hard rocks, which have been wrinkled and bent to make mountains and valleys. Under the crust lies the mantle. Here the rocks are red-hot and soft. The next layer is called the outer core. The rocks here are so hot that they have melted into a liquid.

crust

mantle

outer core

inner core

Scientists think that the very middle of the Earth is 60 times hotter than boiling water.

✳ A solid ball of rock, called the inner core, lies at the centre of the Earth.

❋ The Earth is surrounded by a layer of air called the atmosphere. Air contains important gases such as oxygen, which we breathe to keep us alive.

❋ The atmosphere keeps us warm by trapping the heat of the Sun. It also stops some of the Sun's harmful rays from reaching the ground.

❋ The atmosphere has several different layers. Higher up, the air gets thinner and colder, and there is less oxygen to breathe. In the highest layers there is hardly any air at all.

satellite

space shuttle

air gets
thinner

gas balloon

hot-air
balloon

aircraft

The weather

✳ The weather is what is going on in the air above us. It can be hot or cold, wet or dry, windy or still.

✳ Rain is water that falls from clouds. As the Sun warms the sea, the sea water turns into a gas called water vapour. This rises and cools, and turns into tiny water droplets. The droplets form a cloud. Winds blow the cloud over the land

water vapour

wind

cloud

RAIN

SEA

✳ The water droplets join and grow heavier, until they fall back to earth as rain. The rainwater eventually runs back to the sea.

snow crystals

※ When it is very cold, the water in clouds may freeze, and fall as snow or hail.

Hurricanes are great storms that can bring winds of up to 200 kilometres an hour and heavy rain. They form over the sea and can cause enormous damage to places on the coast.

※ Wind is moving air. Light winds, such as breezes, move slowly. Strong winds, such as gales, move quickly.

light breeze

strong wind

gale

37

※ Thunderstorms usually occur after very hot weather. There is heavy rain with thunder and lightning. Lightning is a huge electric spark between two storm clouds, or between clouds and the ground. Thunder is the noise made by the spark as it rips through the air.

Climates and seasons

✳ Seasons are the changes in the weather through the year. The climate of a place is the pattern of its weather over many years.

The Mediterranean area is hot and dry in the summer, rainy and warm in winter.

Places with a continental climate have warm summers and very cold winters.

Places on the Equator have only one season – hot and wet.

Desert climates are always very dry.

At the North and South Poles there are two seasons: a long, cold winter and a short summer.

✳ The seasons depend on where the Earth is on its journey around the Sun.

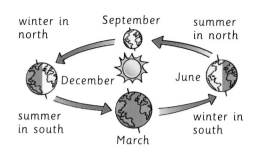

winter in north   September   summer in north

December   June

summer in south   March   winter in south

✳ From March to September, the North Pole is tipped towards the Sun. Places north of the equator have spring and summer, while places south of the equator have autumn and winter.

Places with a coastal climate have warm summers, mild winters and rain all year.

✳ From September to March things are the other way round. It is autumn and winter in the north, spring and summer in the south.

A tropical climate is hot all year round, but there are two seasons: a dry season and a wet one.

Volcanoes and earthquakes

✳ A volcano is a mountain that sometimes erupts, throwing out hot rock and gas from deep in the Earth.

✳ Volcanoes are found where the Earth's crust is thin and cracked. Hot, melted rock (lava) forces its way up from below and blasts out of a crack. As this lava flows away from the crack, it cools and hardens into new rock. This piles up around the crack to form a volcano.

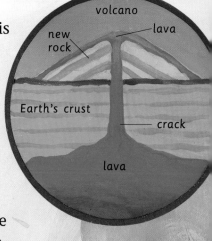

volcano

lava

new rock

Earth's crust

crack

lava

✳ A volcano may not erupt for many years, or it may stop erupting altogether.

✳ Earthquakes under the sea can cause enormous waves called tsunamis. These race to the shore and flood the land.

✳ During an earthquake the ground shakes violently. The surface rocks crumple and tilt, and huge cracks open up. Big earthquakes can cause tremendous damage.

✳ Earthquakes happen when rocks in the Earth's crust move, deep under our feet. Most big earthquakes occur in places along fault lines. These are splits in the Earth's crust.

41

1
2
3
4
5
6
7
8
9
10

The Richter Scale measures the strength of an earthquake. Earthquakes measuring below 4 are not usually felt by people. An earthquake measuring 10 causes huge devastation.

Rocks, metals and minerals

Rocks are the hard, solid parts of the Earth. All rocks are made up of chemicals called minerals.

✳ Igneous rock is formed when hot lava from a volcano cools, and hardens to form rock.

igneous rock

metamorphic rock

igneous rock

metamorphic rock

sedimentary rock

Fossils are the remains of plants and animals found in rocks. From fossils we can learn about the plants and animals that lived millions of years ago.

fossil bird

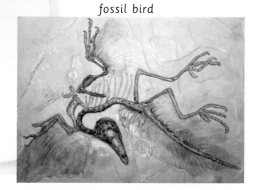

sedimentary rock

✳ Sedimentary rocks are formed from layers of mud, sand or shells at the bottom of rivers, lakes or seas. Over the years, they get squashed into rock.

✳ If rocks become very hot or are squeezed and heated, they may change into different kinds of rocks. These are called metamorphic rocks.

coal mining

43

✳ Many things come from rocks. Fuels such as coal and oil are found in rocks. Pottery is made from clay (a soft rock), baked in a hot oven. Glass is made from special sand and a rock called limestone.

✳ Metals are found in rocks called 'ores'. The ores must be crushed and heated to collect the metal.

✳ Metals such as gold, and minerals like diamonds and rubies, are valuable because they are very rare.

The changing landscape

✳ The shape of the landscape is slowly changing, year by year. Wind, water and cold break down rocks in different ways. And new land is formed from the rock that is worn away.

In hot, dry places, the wind blows sand that scrapes away at rocks and cuts them into strange shapes.

✳ When two pieces of the Earth's crust push into each other, their edges slowly crumple and fold. This is how mountains are made.

new land forming

✳ New land is made by rivers. Fast-flowing rivers carry away rock pieces and break them up further. Near the sea, the rivers slow down, and the rock pieces sink to form new land.

✳ Rain and ice wear away mountains.
Water pours into cracks in rocks. If it freezes,
it expands and splits off
small pieces.

sea wears
away cliffs

✳ The sea's waves pound
on rocky coasts, wearing
them away. Rivers cut away
the land to make valleys
and gorges.

Pollution

Some towns pump waste into rivers or the sea. Factories sometimes release poisonous wastes into water. This can kill fishes and other water life. Farmers use fertilizers on the land that can also pollute rivers.

✳ Waste from cars, homes and factories pours into the air, rivers and seas around us. The waste causes pollution, which can damage and kill plants and animals. It can also harm us.

46

✳ When we burn fuel, we make the air dirtier. The layer of dirty air around the Earth traps more of the Sun's heat, and the Earth gets warmer. This is called the 'greenhouse effect'.

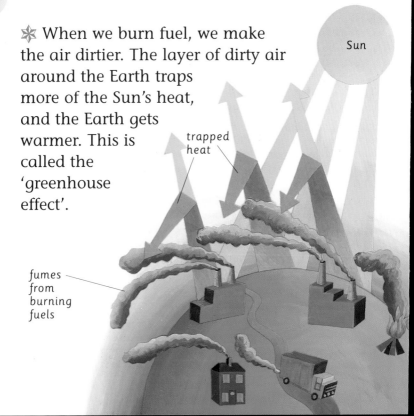

Sun

trapped heat

fumes from burning fuels

Animals and Plants

What are plants?

Plants come in all shapes and sizes, from tiny mosses to huge trees. Many plants have flowers and produce seeds. The seeds will become new plants.

Plants make their own food in their leaves. They use energy from sunlight, water and a gas called carbon dioxide from the air. The process is called photosynthesis.

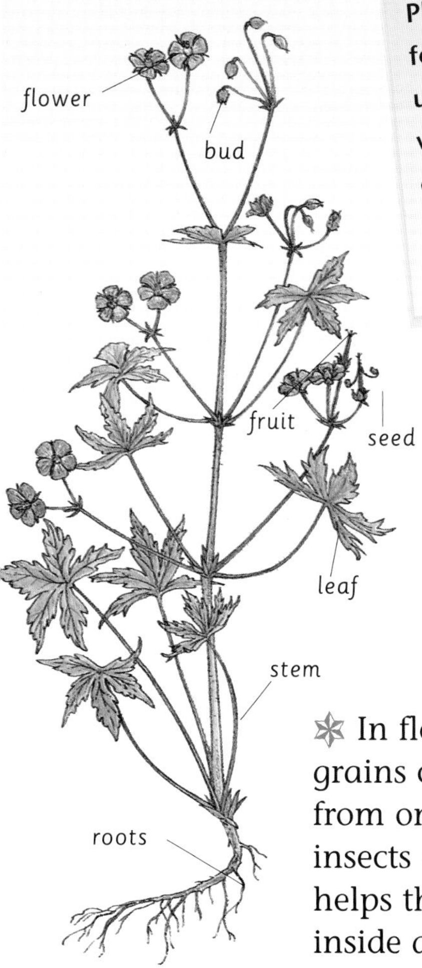
flower
bud
fruit
seed
leaf
stem
roots

Flowering plants have roots that take up water and hold the plant firmly in the ground. The stem supports the leaves, flowers and fruit.

In flowering plants, tiny grains called pollen are carried from one flower to another by insects or the wind. The pollen helps the flower to form seeds, inside a fruit.

Plant families

❋ There are more than 400,000 different kinds of plant. Many are flowering plants, but others do not have flowers.

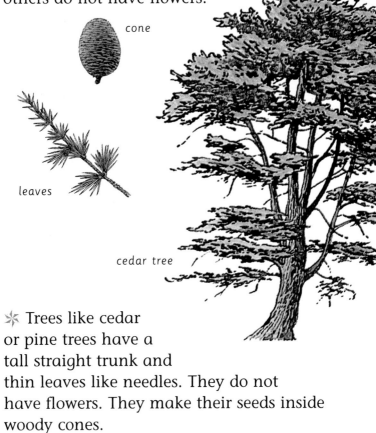

cone

leaves

cedar tree

❋ Trees like cedar or pine trees have a tall straight trunk and thin leaves like needles. They do not have flowers. They make their seeds inside woody cones.

❋ Most of the simpler kinds of plants, like algae, mosses and ferns, do not have flowers or produce seeds. Instead, they reproduce

seaweed

using tiny, dust-like spores.

✳ The largest algae are seaweeds.
The smallest are tiny
and can only
be seen with a
microscope.

fern

moss

✳ A moss is a very
simple kind of plant.
Mosses live in moist
places on land.

✳ Ferns have roots, stems and
leaves. They usually live in damp
places on land. Ferns have leaves,
or fronds, that are made up of
many small leaflets.

To grow your own plants, soak some paper
towels in water and put them on a saucer.
Sprinkle some seeds (mustard or
cress are the easiest) on top, and
put the saucer on a sunny
window-sill. Make sure the
towels stay damp. Your seeds
will soon start to sprout.

Animal families

✳ There are probably more than 10 million different species of animal.

✳ Mammals are the only animals with fur or hair. All mammals drink milk from their mothers when they are young. Bats, whales and monkeys are mammals – and so are you!

chimpanzee

✳ Birds are the only animals with feathers. They are born from eggs. Birds have strong wings, but some birds, like the ostrich and the penguin, cannot fly.

blue tit

✳ Most reptiles live on dry land. Their skin is covered with tough, dry scales. Lizards, snakes, crocodiles and turtles are all reptiles.

cobra

❋ Amphibians are born in the water, but when they grow up, they can live on land. Frogs, toads and newts are all amphibians.

salmon

❋ Fishes live in water. Their bodies are covered in scales and they have fins to help them swim. Fish breathe through gills.

❋ Arthropods do not have bones. Instead they have a hard skin or shell on the outside of their body. Arthropods have at least three pairs of legs. Insects are the most common arthropods.

spider

oil beetle

❋ Molluscs have a soft body, with a hard shell around it. Molluscs have no legs, but many have a kind of 'foot' to help them move about. An octopus is a mollusc with its shell inside its body.

blue-ringed octopus

Prehistoric life

✳ The first living things developed in the sea over 3,500 million years ago.

single-cell animals

✳ Some of the earliest creatures were simple water plants called algae.

algae

200

jellyfish

100

52

giant ferns

trilobites

✳ Plants and some insects began to live on land around 400 million years ago.

50

first fish with jaws

first amphibians

40

first reptiles

30

first mammals

flying insects

20

first dinosaurs

first humans

first birds

first apes

10

present day

✳ As fish became bigger, they grew bony skeletons. Some fish used their fins to drag themselves out of the water. They developed into amphibians, which lived partly on land.

✳ Around 280 million years ago some of these amphibians developed into land-living reptiles, and later dinosaurs. Reptiles such as the pterosaurs took to the air. Mammals and birds were the last kinds of animal to appear.

pterosaur

✳ More than 1,000 different kinds of dinosaur existed. Some were enormous. The brachiosaur was as big as five elephants, and the tyrannosaur was one of the biggest meat-eating animals that has ever lived.

The last dinosaurs died out suddenly 64 million years ago. No one knows why they disappeared. But some scientists believe that birds are descended from dinosaurs.

tyrannosaur

Wildlife in towns

✳ In gardens and parks, birds make their nests in trees and hedges. Housemartins make their nests under the edge of a roof. Coal tits like nesting boxes.

✳ Earthworms burrow in the soil, which they eat to get tiny scraps of food. A football pitch may contain half a tonne of earthworms. Gardeners don't like slugs, but they mostly eat decaying plants.

✳ Many animals live inside your home without you knowing it. Mice, cockroaches and flies like houses because they are warm and it is easy to find food. Spiders spin webs in dark corners, while beetle grubs bore holes in wood.

poppy

wren

garden spider

starling

If you want to watch animals in the garden, find a stone and turn it over. Remember to put the stone back afterwards.

pupa

peacock butterfly

caterpillar

egg

✳ Butterflies are familiar garden insects. Their eggs hatch into caterpillars, which feed on leaves. When it is big enough, a caterpillar grows a hard shell, and becomes a pupa. Inside the pupa, the caterpillar changes. Eventually an adult butterfly comes out.

foxglove

robin

chaffinch

blackbirds

sparrow

✳ Many foxes live in wild corners of towns and cities. They come out at night, looking for food in dustbins or on rubbish tips.

✳ Gardens and parks are full of beautiful plants. They also attract many birds, especially when people put up nesting boxes or bird tables.

Meadows

☀ In a meadow you can find field mice, rabbits and birds. There are also insects such as butterflies, beetles and bees.

kestrel

☀ Kestrels hover in the air above meadows. They swoop down on small animals such as voles.

skylark

yellowhammer

honey bee

orchid

rabbit

poppy

crow

butterfly

vole

field mouse

frog

☀ Moles dig long tunnels under the ground, looking for worms. They can eat their own weight of earthworms in a day.

mole

Woodland

❈ Woodland trees are home for many birds and insects. Larger animals, such as deer and bears, shelter beneath the trees.

An ants' nest may contain over 100,000 ants. But it is started by just one ant – the queen. She lays all the eggs.

woodpecker

57

❈ In autumn, black bears look for somewhere to sleep through the winter ahead. Sleeping helps them to live through the cold months, when there is little food.

❈ Autumn is also when the leaves fall from the trees and start to rot. Millions of worms and beetles chew up the leaves and help mix them with the soil.

black bear

ground beetle

millipede

earthworm

Grasslands

✳ There are grasslands in many parts of the world. The grasslands of North America are called the prairies. The dry grasslands of central Asia are called the steppes.

gazelle

zebra

wildebeeste

locust

savannah grass

✳ Some of the world's largest animals live on the savannah, the grasslands of East Africa. Herds of zebra, wildebeeste and gazelle feed side by side on the grass, which can grow up to three metres tall.

The cheetah is the fastest of all land animals. It can run at more than 80 kilometres an hour, for short bursts. It can easily catch a gazelle or an antelope.

termite
mound

lion

❋ On the savannah, lions and cheetahs hunt the zebras and gazelles. Any meat they leave is quickly finished up by jackals and vultures.

❋ Grasslands have many small animals, too. Birds eat the grass seeds. Beetles munch the dead leaves. Huge mounds, twice as tall as a person, are built by millions of tiny termites.

Giraffes and elephants chew the leaves or twigs of the tough, thorny trees. Giraffes use their long necks to reach the highest branches.

Rainforests

harpy eagle

✳ Rainforests are home to more plants and animals than any other place on Earth. Each layer of the forest has different animals and plants living there.

spider monkey

✳ The tops of the larger trees form a kind of roof over the forest. This is called the canopy. Most animals, including insects, birds and monkeys, live up among the leaves. Other plants grow on the trees, too.

macaw

The rainforests are in serious danger! People are cutting down huge areas for wood and for farming. Every second, an area the size of a football pitch is cut down. Soon many plants and animals will become extinct – they will be gone forever.

anaconda

❉ The poison-arrow frog carries her tadpoles on her back up a tree. She leaves them in a puddle of rainwater collected in the cup-shaped leaves of a plant called a bromeliad.

toucan

❉ Sloths hang upside-down from the branches. They move very slowly.

61

❉ On the rainforest floor it is damp, dark and very hot. Only a few animals, such as jaguars and snakes, live on the ground.

sloth

jaguar

Deserts

✳ Deserts are areas where it hardly ever rains. The land is usually bare rocks, gravel or sand. Most deserts are very hot in the day, but at night they quickly cool down.

cactus

✳ Most animals avoid the fierce heat of the day. The fennec fox and the gerbil hide under rocks or in burrows, where it is much cooler. At night, the animals come out to hunt for food.

fennec fox

✳ The sand becomes scorching hot during the day, but desert creatures find ways of moving about. The sidewinder snake moves so that only a small part of its body touches the sand at a time. The skink swims through the sand by wriggling its body.

skink

✳ Some desert plants store water in their stems or roots. Cacti have tiny spines instead of leaves so that they do not lose water. The leaves of esparto grass curl up to keep in water.

✳ The adult sand grouse has spongy feathers on its breast. When it is nesting, it flies many miles to find water. Then it soaks it breast feathers and flies back to the nest. The young suck the water from the feathers.

esparto grass

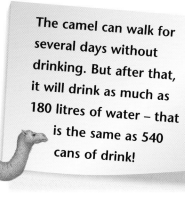

The camel can walk for several days without drinking. But after that, it will drink as much as 180 litres of water – that is the same as 540 cans of drink!

The Arctic

✳ The Arctic lands (the tundra) are free of ice and snow for only a few months each year. In the short summer, the ice and snow melt, plants flower, insects lay eggs and animals mate and find food.

✳ Many animals come to the tundra just for the summer. Caribou arrive in huge herds to feed on leaves and lichen. Birds come to eat mosquitoes and other insects that hatch in the boggy pools.

caribou

The Arctic tern travels further than any other bird. It rears its young near the North Pole, then migrates 18,000 kilometres to the South Pole for the southern summer.

✳ In winter, the Arctic fox grows a thick, white coat. This makes the fox difficult to see against the snow. In summer, its coat turns brown again.

Musk oxen protect themselves against wolves by standing in a circle, with their long curved horns facing outwards.

musk oxen

wolf

✳ The main plants that grow on the tundra are mosses, grasses and lichens. The Arctic willow is one of the few trees. It grows close to the ground, sheltered from the icy winds.

snowy owl

✳ Lemmings spend the winter in burrows under the snow. In the summer, they have to beware of snowy owls and other hunters.

lemming

Oceans

✳ The world's oceans are full of microscopic plants and animals called plankton. Plankton are food for many other sea animals.

✳ Sea anemones look like plants, but are in fact animals. They have special stinging tentacles, which they use to catch small fish. Clown fish are immune to the anenome's sting, and live among its tentacles.

sea anemone

clown fish

A flesh-eating shark may have up to 3,000 teeth.

✳ Whales are mammals, just like us. They live all their lives in water. The blue whale is the largest animal in the world, but it lives on tiny plankton.

blue whale

Science

Solids, liquids and gases

✳ Everything in the world is either a solid, a liquid or a gas. Solids have a fixed shape. Liquids have no fixed shape and you can pour them. Gases fill any space they are put into.

metal (solid)

milk (liquid)

air in balloon (gas)

ice

water

✳ Heating and cooling materials can change them. Ice is a solid. If it gets warm it turns into a liquid – water. If you heat water so that it boils, it turns into a gas – steam. If steam touches something cold, it cools and turns into water. Put the water in the freezer and it will turn back into ice.

steam

Atoms and molecules

✳ Everything is made of matter. All matter is made of very tiny particles called atoms. Just one grain of salt contains billions of atoms.

✳ An element is a substance that is made from just one kind of atom. There are over 100 different elements. Most are metals.

sodium

✳ Elements join together in many ways to make millions of different substances. Salt, for example, is made of sodium and chlorine atoms.

chlorine

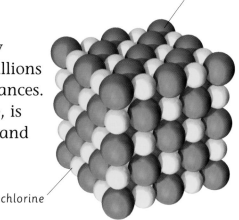

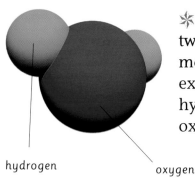

✳ A molecule consists of two or more atoms. A molecule of water, for example, consists of two hydrogen atoms and one oxygen atom.

hydrogen

oxygen

✳ We use different kinds of matter in different ways. For example, the frame of a bicycle is made of metal, which is strong. Rubber, which is springy, is used for the tyres. Clothes are made of materials that are soft and flexible.

clothes
(cotton)

frame
(metal)

tyres
(rubber)

Energy

✳ There are many different kinds of energy. A car gets energy from petrol, a computer gets energy from electricity. A sailing ship gets energy from the wind. You get your energy from food.

Sun

heat and light

grass

milk

✳ Almost all the energy we use comes originally from the Sun. Grass uses the Sun's energy to grow. Cows eat the grass and turn some of the energy from it into milk. If you drink the milk, the energy passes into your body.

The energy from one litre of petrol will drive a car about 16 kilometres. If you used the same amount of energy on a bicycle, you could cycle over 500 kilometres!

16 km

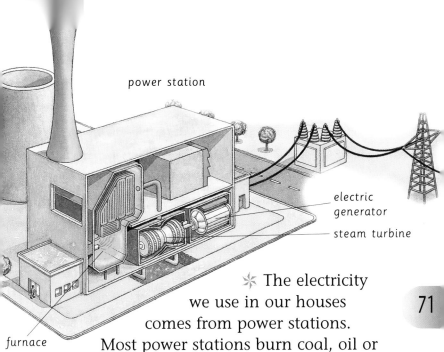

power station

electric generator

steam turbine

furnace

✳ The electricity we use in our houses comes from power stations. Most power stations burn coal, oil or gas to heat water and make steam. The steam turns giant machines which make electricity.

hydroelectric power

wind power

✳ Electricity can also be made using energy from the wind or water. In hydroelectric power stations, rushing water turns the machines to produce electricity. In wind farms special windmills make electricity. Solar panels make electricity from sunlight.

solar panel

Forces

✳ If you push or pull something it moves. Pushing and pulling are forces. A force can make objects start to move, speed up, slow down, stop, or travel in a different direction.

✳ A force called gravity pulls everything on the Earth towards the ground. When you kick a ball into the air, it comes down again. Even when you stand still, the gravity of the Earth is pulling you downwards. Without gravity you would float in the air!

✳ Friction is a force that tries to stop things sliding over another. Friction between your shoes and the floor stops you from slipping over. But on ice there is less friction, so you can slide along.

✳ Magnets attract things made of iron or steel, such as paper clips or nails. This is called magnetic force. A magnet has two ends, or poles,

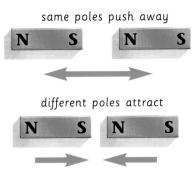

same poles push away

different poles attract

called north (N) and south (S). The north poles of two magnets will push away from each other. South poles do this, too. But the north pole of one magnet and the south pole of another attract each other.

The Earth acts like a giant magnet. It has a magnetic north pole and a magnetic south pole.

Light and sound

✳ Light is a kind of energy. It comes from the Sun, from fire or from electricity. It travels very fast – one million kilometres in three seconds.

✳ Light travels in straight lines, called rays. When light rays hit a shiny surface, they bounce back, or are reflected. When light bounces off your body and hits a shiny mirror, it is reflected back to you and you see a picture of yourself.

Light is really a mixture of colours. When light passes through a triangular-shaped piece of glass, called a prism, it breaks up into separate colours. These are called the colours of the spectrum.

✳ Rainbows are formed when the Sun shines while it is raining. Each raindrop acts as a tiny prism, splitting up the light into many colours.

spectrum

prism

✳ Sounds are made by vibrations pushing the air about. The vibrations in the air are sound waves. To make sounds, we make the air in our throats vibrate. The faster the vibrations, the higher the sound.

✳ The loudest sound recorded was caused by a volcano. When the volcanic island of Krakatoa erupted in 1883, the bang was heard clearly 5,000 km away.

Sound waves travel through air more slowly than light but still very fast – one kilometre in three seconds.

✳ The loudness of sounds is measured in decibels (dB).

Type of sound	dB
Damage to hearing	140
Jet taking off	130
	120
Rock concert	110
Loud radio	100
Heavy traffic	90
	80
	70
Conversation	60
	50
	40
Whisper	30
The quietest sound you can hear	20
	10

Electricity

✳ Electricity powers many things in your home – your television and your washing machine, for example.

power station

homes

factory

✳ Most of the electricity we use comes from huge buildings called power stations. The electricity travels along thick wires to factories, shops, schools and homes.

bulb

wire

battery

switch

✳ Batteries also make electricity. When you connect a bulb to a battery with a wire, the bulb lights up. Electrical energy flows along the wire to the bulb. The bulb only lights up if it is connected in a circle back to the battery. This is called a circuit.

NEVER touch bare wires or electric sockets or plugs. You could get an electric shock. Always ask a grown-up to help you when you use electricity.

Technology

Raw materials

✳ Raw materials are materials that we get out of the ground or from plants and animals. We use them to make new materials.
For example, wood from trees is the raw material for paper.

iron ore

furnace

✳ Iron comes from a rock called iron ore. The ore is broken up and heated in a furnace to make iron. Iron is heated with other materials to make steel, a very strong metal.

iron

steel furnace

steel

✳ Wool comes from the coats of sheep, goats or other animals. It can be knitted to make clothes or woven to make cloth. Cotton comes from a living plant.

✳ Oil is the raw material for plastic. Hot plastic is a thick liquid, which can be squashed or moulded into thousands of different shapes.

paper

wood

plastic

steel

wool

Building and engineering

✳ Huge structures like skyscrapers, tunnels and bridges need to be made of strong materials, such as concrete and steel. They also need skilled engineers to make sure they are safe.

✳ Skyscrapers need very firm foundations to support the heavy weight of the building – concrete and steel are sunk into the earth. A framework of concrete or steel holds up the skyscraper. Panels of light metal or glass cover the framework on the outside.

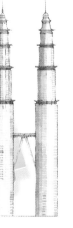

The tallest skyscrapers in the world are the two Petronas Towers in Kuala Lumpur, Malaysia. They are 452 metres high.

suspension bridge

✳ Bridges carry roads and railways over valleys or rivers. They must be able to support heavy loads. The longest bridges are usually suspension bridges. In a suspension bridge, the road hangs from steel cables.

✳ Tunnels allow roads and railways to pass through mountains, under rivers and even under seas. Engineers use a special tunnelling machine for digging through soft rock. To tunnel through hard rocks, they use explosives.

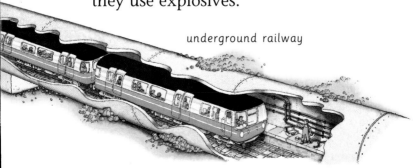

underground railway

Machines

✳ Machines help us to do an amazing number of things. Some machines are very simple.

✳ Wheels make it much easier to move a heavy weight a long way.

wheelbarrow

✳ You can use a lever to lift a heavy weight. A lever is a long bar, which rests on a turning point called a 'pivot'. A wheelbarrow is made from a wheel and two levers (the handles).

✳ A wedge has a thin, sharp side and a thick side. If you push the sharp side in between two objects, the thicker part of the wedge gets into the crack. It forces the two objects further apart. A tin opener is made from a wheel (the handle) and a wedge (the cutter).

Oil tankers are probably the biggest machines ever made. Some of these ships are so long that they have room for five football pitches on deck!

tin opener

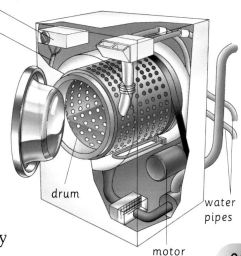

control box
electricity supply
drum
water pipes
motor

✳ Washing machines, lawnmowers and cars are more complex machines.
A washing machine can wash clothes better than you can. All it needs is water, detergent and electricity

81

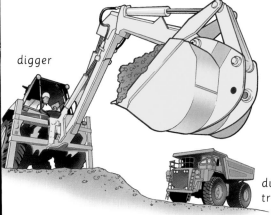

digger

dumper truck

✳ Even bigger machines, such as diggers and trucks, help to build buildings and roads.

✳ Robots are machines that can work by themselves. A computer controls them. In car factories, robots help to put cars together.

Transport

✳ Cars, buses, lorries, trains, ships and aeroplanes are our main ways of getting about. They carry people and things from place to place.

TGV

✳ The earliest railway engines were driven by steam. Today's trains have diesel engines, or are powered by electricity. The fastest train in the world is the French TGV.

ocean liner

✳ Before engines were invented, all ships had sails. They used the wind to move them along. Big modern ships have diesel engines, powered by burning oil.

✳ The bicycle is one of the most popular forms of transport in the world. When you pedal, a system of toothed wheels and a chain make the back wheel turn and move you forwards.

radar in nose cone

flight deck

❄ There are more than 500 million cars in the world today. The first motor car had no roof and hard seats. Modern cars are roomy and comfortable.

people carrier

❄ Early aeroplanes were driven along by propellers. Modern aircraft have jet engines. Air and hot gases shoot out of the back of the engine, pushing the plane forwards

galley (kitchen)

passenger area

fuel tank

jet engine

Airbus airliner

space shuttle

❄ Spacecraft use rocket engines. These are the only engines that work in space.

Communications

✳ Communications are ways in which we keep in touch with each other. We communicate over long distances using letters, telephones, television, radio, fax and e-mail.

✳ A TV camera changes the pictures it sees into electrical signals. These travel down a wire to a transmitting aerial on top of a tall mast. The aerial sends the signals out in all directions as radio waves. An aerial on your house picks up the signals and your television changes them back into pictures.

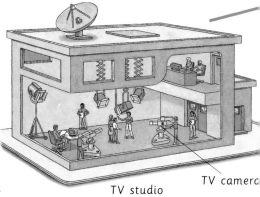

TV studio

TV camera

✳ When you speak into the mouthpiece of a telephone, your words are turned into an electric signal. The signal travels down a wire to the person you are calling.

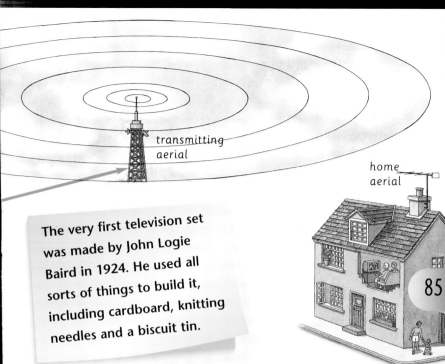

transmitting aerial

home aerial

The very first television set was made by John Logie Baird in 1924. He used all sorts of things to build it, including cardboard, knitting needles and a biscuit tin.

85

✳ Today many people have mobile phones. These use microwaves to send messages.

✳ E-mail is short for electronic mail. It is a way of sending letters between computers.

✳ Satellites high above the Earth can pass on telephone, radio and television signals across the world.

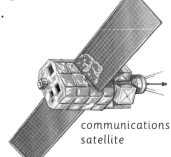

communications satellite

Computers

✳ Lots of things we use every day have a computer inside them. For example, many cars have computers that help the engine work.

microprocessor

✳ At the heart of every computer is a tiny electronic circuit called a 'microprocessor'. The microprocessor does all the calculations and carries out the instructions it gets from the computer's programs.

86

✳ We tell a computer what to do by typing on the keyboard or by clicking the mouse.

monitor

✳ We use computers in our homes, schools, businesses and shops. You can use them to write and draw, do sums, play games and send electronic mail.

keyboard

printer

disks

The Universe

The Solar System

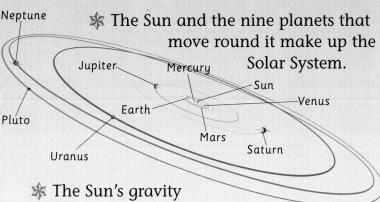

✳ The Sun and the nine planets that move round it make up the Solar System.

Neptune
Jupiter
Mercury
Sun
Venus
Earth
Pluto
Mars
Saturn
Uranus

✳ The Sun's gravity pulls on all the planets and keeps them in their place. Mercury is the nearest planet to the Sun – and one of the hottest. Venus and Earth are the next closest. Then come Mars, Jupiter, Saturn, Uranus, Neptune and, furthest away of all, Pluto.

✳ Mercury, Venus, Mars and Earth are rocky planets. Jupiter, Saturn, Uranus and Neptune are made up mainly of gas.

Jupiter is the largest planet, and Pluto the smallest. Jupiter is eleven times bigger across the middle than Earth, and over 300 times heavier.

Jupiter

Earth

• Pluto

The Sun and the Moon

✵ The Earth is a planet that travels round the Sun. It takes a year (about 365 days) to go all the way round once. At the same time, the Moon travels round the Earth. It takes 28 days (about one month) to go round once.

Moon

✵ The Sun is a giant ball of very hot gases. Huge fiery flames shoot out from its surface. The flames are thousands of kilometres high.

✵ The Sun is 150 million kilometres from Earth. The temperature of the Sun at its centre is about 15 million °C. The surface is about 9,000 °C. Dark sunspots sometimes appear on the surface. These areas are cooler than the rest of the Sun.

sunspot

Never look directly at the Sun. Its light is so bright it could blind you.

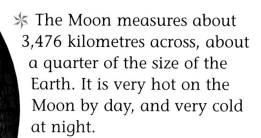

✳ The Moon measures about 3,476 kilometres across, about a quarter of the size of the Earth. It is very hot on the Moon by day, and very cold at night.

✳ The surface of the Moon is made up of mountains, craters and great dusty plains called seas. Some mountains are over 600 metres high. The largest craters are over 290 kilometres across. There is no life on the Moon.

| full (or new) Moon | three-quarter Moon | half Moon | crescent Moon | Moon completely hidden |

✳ The Moon does not really shine. Moonlight is light from the Sun reflected off the surface of the Moon. The Sun always lights up half the Moon. But as the Moon travels round the Earth, we see different amounts of its bright side. This is why the Moon seems to change shape.

The stars

✳ A star is a glowing ball of gas that gives out lots of heat and light.

star-forming cloud

✳ Stars are formed from moving clouds of dust and gas in space. If part of a cloud begins to shrink, the gas is crushed tightly into a ball, and becomes very, very hot. One day it becomes so hot that it starts to shine brightly as a new star.

Milky Way

✳ A galaxy is an enormous group of stars. We belong to a galaxy called the Milky Way, which forms a misty band across the sky. Astronomers believe that altogether the Milky Way contains 100,000 million stars.

❊ When you look at stars, they seem to twinkle. In fact, a star gives out steady beams of light. The twinkling effect is caused by moving air in the Earth's atmosphere, which bends and breaks up the beams.

❊ Some bright stars make shapes in the sky. These are called constellations. The shapes can look like animals, or like people. One of the easiest star shapes to see in the northern half of the world is Orion the Hunter. You can only see it in the winter

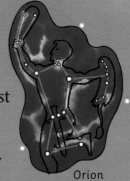

Orion

Hubble space telescope

❊ We can look far into space using telescopes. In 1990, scientists sent a telescope up into space to get an even clearer look. It is called the Hubble Space Telescope. It has sent us back some amazing photographs.

Exploring space

helmet

backpack controls

protective spacesuit

astronaut on a space walk

✳ The first spacecraft, *Sputnik 1*, went into orbit round the Earth in 1957. Since that time, thousands of spacecraft have been launched, many carrying astronauts.

✳ In 1969 the *Apollo 11* spacecraft landed the first people on the Moon. They were American astronauts Neil Armstrong and 'Buzz' Aldrin.

✳ A space station is a large spacecraft where people can live and work for months at a time. Astronauts visited the Russian space station *Mir* from 1986 to 1999. Work has now begun on a new International Space Station.

Mir

Apollo 11

jet-powered backpack
and air supply

The first person in space was a Russian, Yuri Gagarin, in 1961.

✳ Satellites circling the Earth are used for communications, weather forecasting and collecting military information.

✳ Probes are unmanned spacecraft that visit other planets. They take pictures and collect information.

✳ In 1976 two *Viking* space probes sent back pictures from Mars. In 1989 the space probe *Voyager 2* flew past Neptune. Earlier on, it had passed Jupiter, Saturn and Uranus.

✳ In 1995 the spacecraft *Galileo* took close-up pictures of Jupiter.

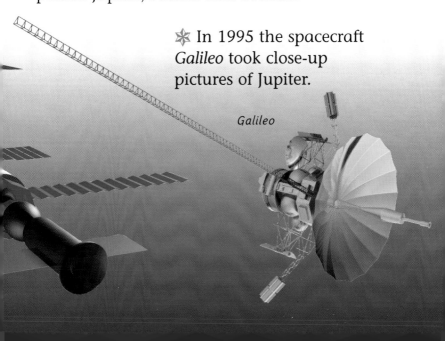

Galileo

Index

Acknowledgements

Illustrations

Key: t = top; c = centre; b = bootom; l = left; r = right; back = background; fore = foreground

Baker, Julian; 22t, c; 23t; 52back, Baum, Julian; 31; 34; 35; 87; 88-89; 91t, back; 92b, Beier, Ellen; 28; 29; 30c, Birkett, Georgie; 25t; 82; 83t, b, Blathwayt, Benedict; 22-23b; 79b, Brown, Chris; 43b, Burton, Andy; 4c; 81b, Butler, Johnathan; 56; 57; 62l; 62-63c; 63t; 64t; 65, Cope, Jane; 72t, Courtney, Michael; 5b; 6c; 6-7t; 8l; 18r; 19t, c, Davies, John; 54b; 55b, Eccles, Tessa; 73c, Edwards, Brinn; 66t, Edwards, Mark; 24; 25b, Gaffney, Michael; 64b, Goodyear, Clive; 9b; 12; 13; 14-15c; 16; 17; 26c, bl; 70c; 76b; 77t; 79t; 80t, br;, Gulbis, Stephen; 76t, Hardy, David; 85br, Haslam, John; 1; 37b; 39t; 67t, cr; 70t; 75br; 85tl; 86b;, Hinks, Gary; 42c; 83c, Howatson, Ian; 4b; 92t, Joyce, Peter; 37t, Lach, Steve; 26br; 27, Lawrence, Joe; 78t, Lewis, Jason; 71t; 84-85t, Lings, Steve; 36; 44-45, Milne, Sean; 51t; 58; 59, Oxford Illustrators; 81t, Oxford University Press; 32-33; 38-39, Parsley, Helen; 43t, Pipes, Alan Fred; 73b, Polley, Robbie; 76b, Richardson, Paul; 50t; 63b, Riley, Terry; 4t; 52 (fore); 53, Ritchie, Scot; 3c; 6b; 7c, b; 15r; 19b; 20b; 21; 30t; 49b; 76cl, b; 70b; 71b; 72b; 73t; 74t; 75bl; 80bl; 86t, Roberts, Steve; 50c, b; 51c; 60; 61; 66br, Saddington, Lesley; 3b; 40-41; 46, Smith, Joshua; 68, Spenceley, Annabel; 30b; 75t, Tamblin, Treve; 51b; bl, Visscher, Peter; 47; 48; 49tr, tl, c; 55t, Weston, Steve; 3t; 8-9c; 10-11t, b; 18l, Willey, Lynne; 11b; 20t, c; 69; 77b
Woods, Michael/Gecko Ltd; 54t

Photos

The Publishers would like to thank the following for permission to reproduce photographs:
42t Geo Science Features/Dr B. Booth; 42b Corbis Images; 90, 91 NASA